The Manatee

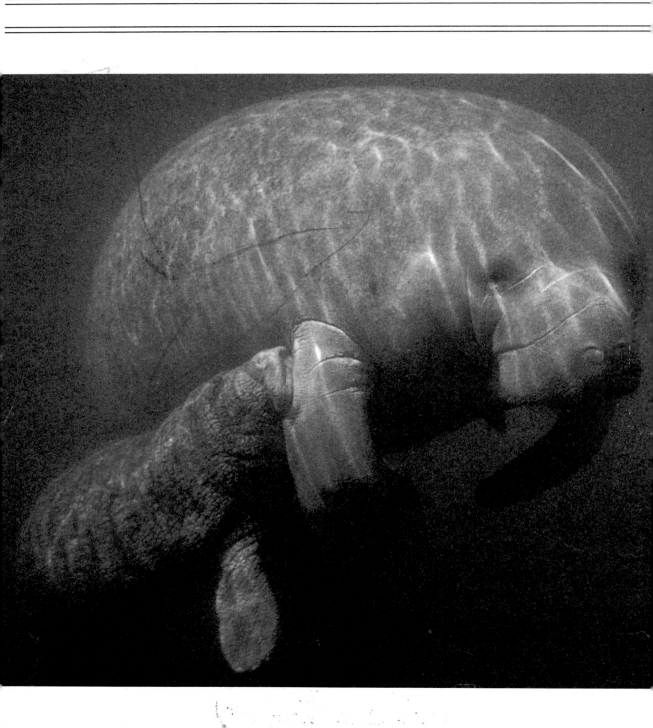

The Manatee

By Jean H. Sibbald

DILLON PRESS, INC.
Minneapolis, Minnesota 55415

Acknowledgments

A special thanks goes to Judith Delaney Vallee of The Save the Manatee Club for reviewing the manuscript, and to Patrick Rose for supplying photographs for the book. The photographs are reproduced through the courtesy of the Florida Marine Research Institute, Florida Department of Natural Resources; J.D. Duff Photography; The Save the Manatee Club (Patrick M. Rose, photographer); Jean H. Sibbald; and the U.S. Fish and Wildlife Service (James Powell and Gaylan Rathburn, photographers).

Library of Congress Cataloging-in-Publication Data

Sibbald, Jean H.
  The manatee / by Jean H. Sibbald.
    p.   cm.—(A Dillon remarkable animals book)
  Summary: Discusses the appearance and behavior of the manatee and examines its relationship with humans.

  Includes bibliographical references.

  ISBN 0-87518-429-4 (lib. bdg.) : $12.95
  1. Manatees—Juvenile literature.   [1. Manatees.]
I. Title. II. Series.
QL737.S63S53   1990
599 .5'5—dc20   89-26048
                                                            CIP
                                                             AC

Dillon Press, Inc., 242 Portland Avenue South
Minneapolis, Minnesota 55415

Printed in the United States of America
  2 3 4 5 6 7 8 9 10 99 98 97 96 95 94 93 92 91

Contents

Facts about the
West Indian Manatee

Scientific Name: *Trichechus manatus*

Scientific Order: Sirenia

Common Names: Manatee, sea cow

Related Species: Amazonian manatee, West African manatee, dugong (all are known as sea cows and belong to the scientific order Sirenia)

Range: Coastal and inland waterways from Brazil in South America to Virginia in the United States; in winter, most manatees in the United States gather in Florida

Habitat: Shallow, slow-moving freshwater and saltwater areas with plentiful water plants

Description:
Physical Features—Large, rounded body that narrows down to a flat, paddle-shaped tail; two broad flippers with three or four fingernails on each flipper; thick, wrinkled skin; fat, whiskered upper lip
Length—9 to 13 feet (2.7 to 4.0 meters)
Weight—800 to 3,500 pounds (363 to 1,589 kilograms)
Color—Gray or grayish-brown

Behavior: Spends time eating, resting, swimming, and playing; roams hundreds of miles along waterways, usually in small groups or alone; gathers in herds in warm-water areas in winter; is gentle, slow-moving; has no defenses except to flee

Food: Freshwater and saltwater plants; can eat 100 pounds (45.5 kilograms) or more daily

Reproduction: Forms mating herds of one female and several males; female gives birth to one calf (twins are rare) every two or three years

In Florida's warm coastal waters, a manatee rises toward the surface.

Chapter 1

Gentle Giants of Rivers and Seas

November winds chill northern Florida's coastal waters. A huge, fishlike creature glides silently into the Saint John's River. As she journeys toward a warm, inland spring, her plump body looks like a blimplike shadow in the dark water below.

Every minute or two she rises to the surface for air. It is then that the scars become visible. Deep, white marks criss-cross her broad back. Only one creature has this particular pattern of scars—a West Indian manatee named Success.

Since shortly after her birth, Success has made the yearly **migration*** up the river. Her mother first guided her through the twists and turns leading to Blue Spring. Now, as then, clear waters will greet her. Their year-round temperatures of 72°F

*Words in **bold type** are explained in the glossary at the end of this book.

(22°C) will offer safety from the winter's cold.

She must maintain a warm body temperature for, unlike the fish around her, Success is a mammal. Her first food was her mother's milk, and her lungs require her to breathe fresh air. She even has some body hairs. In these ways, she is like the mammals on land.

Success is just one of the manatees that roam warm coastal seas and rivers. The giant mammals reach 9 to 13 feet (2.7 to 4.0 meters) in length, and can weigh more than 3,000 pounds (1,361 kilograms.)

In their watery world, manatees are, by nature, slow and gentle animals. They have no natural enemies, and they hunt no other creatures.

Mermaids and Seacows

Ancient sailors recognized the gentle nature of manatees and their cousins, the dugongs. Far from home and lonely, the sailors watched the creatures at play. Perhaps they saw something almost human

A full-grown manatee can reach 13 feet in length and weigh more than 3,000 pounds.

in sea mammals that hugged each other with flipper arms. The sailors carried home tales of underwater mothers nursing their young. From such sights, stories of mermaids and **sirens**, or sea maidens, likely were born. Today, the scientific name Sirenia is given to the group of animals made up of manatees and dugongs.

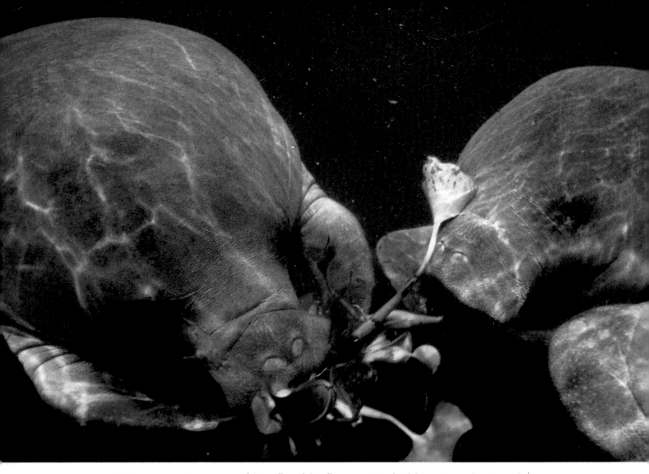

Two manatees use their flexible flippers to hold water plants while they eat.

The gentle creatures are also known as sea cows, for their habit of grazing in pastures of water plants. Like contented cows, they move slowly, munching their way through great fields of sea grasses.

Though manatees may act cowlike, their closest

relatives are elephants. Blood tests and fossil records have shown scientists the connection. Both manatees and elephants have teeth that move forward in their jaws. As the teeth wear down and fall out, new ones replace them from behind. Breeding habits, too, are similar. And both are very large, grayish mammals with a few hairs scattered across their broad bodies.

While the elephant developed a body **adapted**, or suited, for life on land, the manatee adapted to life in the water. Thus, it is called an **aquatic** animal. Only the mammals from one other group are fully aquatic, spending their entire lives in water. That group is made up of the whales, dolphins, and porpoises. They are meat-eaters. The sirenians, or sea cows, are the only plant-eating aquatic mammals.

Adapted for an Aquatic Life

A sirenian is as much at home in the water as any fish. But unlike a fish, it cannot breathe underwater. Every one to five minutes (less often when resting), a manatee lifts its plump, whiskered nose to the surface. Two round, quarter-sized nostrils open wide, releasing stored air with a swooshing sound and taking in fresh air. Flaps of skin snap shut like trap doors to cover the nostrils as they disappear underwater. Sometimes a noisy snort

Viewed from underwater, a manatee lifts its nose to the surface to breathe.

A manatee's nostrils open wide above the surface as it breathes.

and a stream of spray erupts, as if the creature is blowing its nose.

The rounded curves of the manatee's body allow it to move easily through the water. Power for swimming comes from its strong, paddle-shaped tail. Its two broad flippers help in steering, turning,

15

The manatee's paddle-shaped tail and rounded body give it power for swimming.

and moving forward and backward.

Flippers also serve as the manatee's hands and arms. With them, the creature walks along the bottom, or pulls itself up to nibble on land plants at the water's edge. It clutches and holds all kinds of objects—plants, poles, bottles, even a human diver's

16

leg. It can hold food to its mouth or shove it in, and then clean unwanted bits from its lips and gums, all with its flexible flippers. And when a manatee has an itch on its face or chest, it scratches with its fingernails. Three or four dot the tip of each flipper.

How well can a manatee see? How well can it hear? These are questions scientists try to answer. Studies have shown that, underwater, the manatee can see at least as far as a human diver with a mask can. But it probably has difficulty seeing nearby objects clearly through its deep-set eyes. Instead, it explores these with its lips and mouth.

Sound is important in the manatee's world. In dark or cloudy waters, squeaks and squeals keep the animals in touch with each other, especially the mothers and their calves. Though its ear openings are almost invisible, the manatee probably hears well. Sudden sounds, such as a bird plunging into the water, can startle it into fleeing. If there is no danger, however, the curious manatee soon returns to investigate the cause of the sound.

Sea Cows Around the World

Four different **species**, or kinds, of sea cows live in today's world. As with other living things, each species has been given a Latin name that forms the second part of its scientific name. It identifies the species for scientists throughout the world. The first part of the scientific name refers to the genus, or larger group, to which the species belongs. Common names, such as West Indian manatee, dugong, and sea cow, may be different in different languages or areas.

The West Indian manatee is at home along seacoasts from Brazil in South America to the southeastern United States. Scientists have named it *Trichechus manatus*. In the United States, its major home is Florida. But summer wanderings may take it as far west as Louisiana and as far north as Virginia.

South America is also the home of the Amazonian manatee, or *Trichechus inunguis*. This smooth-skinned species stays in the fresh waters of the mighty Amazon River and its many branches.

18   A plant dangles from the mouth of a West Indian manatee along the Florida coast.

Not much is known about the West African manatee, which lives along the coasts and rivers of western Africa. Scientists call it *Trichechus senegalensis*.

The fourth sea cow is the dugong. Its scientific name—*Dugong dugon*—is easy to remember. The creature is slimmer than manatees, and its tail is notched in the middle, rather than rounded. There are also a few other differences, but one look at the dugong's blubbery face clearly shows that it is a sirenian.

Living only in salt water, dugongs are at home along certain coasts from southern Asia to the northern half of Australia. Some are also found along the eastern coast of Africa.

The Sea Cow That Disappeared

In 1741, sailors who were shipwrecked near Alaska discovered herds of a strange kind of sea cow. It later became known as Steller's sea cow, or *Hydrodamalis gigas*. Twice as large as the sea cows of today, it had adapted to the icy seas. Its huge body floated at the surface of shallow waters, making it easy to capture.

For sailors battling winter cold and starvation, the meat of the strange animal was life-saving. It was also delicious. Months later, after rebuilding their ship, the sailors returned home and told others of their discovery. At that time, about 2,000 of the creatures lived in northern waters. They did not last long. Fur hunters and whaling ships caught them for food. Twenty-seven years later, not a single Steller's sea cow remained!

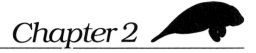

Chapter 2

A Wandering Life

In its warm water world, the manatee lives a wandering life. Its **habitat** ranges from salty coastal waters to freshwater rivers and springs. Within these areas, the gentle giant may travel hundreds of miles in a season—exploring here, stopping to eat there, resting almost anywhere. At 2 to 6 miles (3.2 to 9.7 kilometers) an hour, the journey is a slow one. If the need arises, though, the manatee can make short dashes of 15 miles (24 kilometers) an hour.

Food, water temperatures, and the manatee's own curious nature determine where it goes. Regular coastal routes wind between sandbars and small islands. Sidetrips are many, because manatees explore any likely waterway.

Estuaries, in particular, are favorite cruising

Manatees wander in search of food and warm water, from coastal waters to freshwater rivers and springs.

23

areas. In these protected inlets and bays, fresh water flowing from rivers and streams mixes with the salty waters of the sea.

Hundreds of other creatures share the shallow, plant-rich estuaries. Snails, clams, crabs, shrimp, seabirds, and many kinds of fish abound. The manatee ignores these neighbors, unless a fish insists on being a pest as it pecks at the giant's hide.

Manatees can eat, rest, play, or swim any time of the day or night. They may spend weeks or even months in one place, or move on from day to day.

Except in winter gathering places, or when mating, they are seldom seen in large herds. More often they wander in twos or threes, or even alone. Only the mothers and their calves seem to stay together for long periods of time. Even after being on their own, calves may return to their mother's sides to travel for a time.

Each manatee seems to have its own favorite summer and winter ranges, or areas in which it travels. Bulls roam the greatest distances. As mana-

Algae cover much of the body of this manatee.

tees travel, their bodies often gather a patchy coating of **algae**, or tiny water plants. In salt water, hard-shelled **barnacles** may also settle on their rough, ridged skin. These soon die and drop off in fresh water, though.

When air and water temperatures are warm,

the West Indian manatee makes its most northern journeys. As temperatures begin to dip, the migration to warmer places begins. Most manatees that have roamed northward return to Florida waters. Those that don't rarely survive the cold.

Rivers and springs with year-round temperatures of 72°F (22°C) are among the manatees' favorite places to spend the winter. There are other places, though, where the warm waters are not a work of nature. They flow, instead, from large electric power plants into inlets and bays. Hundreds of manatees have discovered these warm-water outflows, and seek them out in winter.

Wherever it wanders, the manatee spends almost a quarter of its time eating. It is a giant with an appetite to match.

A Plant Diet with Extras

The manatee is **herbivorous**. That is the scientific way of saying it eats plants. A grown manatee needs as much as 100 pounds (45.5 kilograms) of

plant food daily. That is like eating two to three bathtubs full of spinach a day.

Most of the front of the manatee's blunt snout is covered by its fat, muscular upper lip. Whiskers as stiff as the bristles on a hair brush cover the lip, which is divided in the middle. The two sides move

In winter, manatees gather in the warm water flowing from an electric power plant.

almost like hands when they grasp plants and funnel them into the mouth. Soft crunching sounds fill the water as the manatee's flat side teeth, or molars, chew and grind. It has no teeth in front. Intestines as long as two semitrailers digest the huge amounts of food.

Grazing along the bottom, the manatee nips off leaves or digs into the sand to pull out rich, filling roots. Uneaten bits dribble into the water and float away. As the manatee surfaces for air, leaves or stalks may dangle from its mouth. Barely pausing in its chewing, the manatee takes a quick breath, then returns to its meal.

Dense forests of tall water weeds may be attacked in the middle. The manatee tunnels into them, eating as it goes. It pulls floating plants beneath the surface, sometimes holding them carefully between its flippers. At times, the manatee pokes its head out of the water to grab shoreside grasses or even the overhanging leaves of trees.

Hidden among the strands and leaves of the

While feeding, manatees pull floating plants beneath the surface.

manatee's food are many tiny creatures. Worms, leeches, and insects find shelter there. So do baby crabs, starfish, shrimp, and shellfish. As their plant homes are swept into the manatee's mouth, so are they. In this way, the manatee gets some meat along with its vegetables.

A cow and calf feed together. The calf stays with its mother for almost two years.

A Time for New Life

In the world of the West Indian manatee, there is no set season for breeding. When a cow is ready to mate, a herd of bulls soon surrounds her. As many as a dozen or more follow her every move for a week, or as long as a month.

In their excitement, the males forget their normally mild behavior. They push and shove and jostle to be close to the cow. They squeak and groan as their great bodies bump into each other. The cow rolls away from them and may thrash the water with her tail. But no real fights occur.

When the time is right, the cow mates quickly with several bulls. Soon, life returns to normal for the bulls, until another cow is ready for mating.

In about thirteen months, the cow gives birth to a calf. The baby will need its mother's care for almost two years. At least two years will pass before the cow mates again, unless her calf dies. Then the time can be sooner.

As with human babies, newborn manatees vary in size. Their average length is about 4 feet (1.2 meters), and they weigh around 66 pounds (30 kilograms). Rarely, twins are born. Sometimes a manatee will adopt another's calf and care for it along with her own. All are born to a wandering life.

Chapter 3

Can the Manatee Survive?

For millions of years, sea cows roamed coastal areas and rivers in peace. They had no natural enemies. Then, people appeared. They hunted the creature for food, made leather from its skin, used its oil, and ground its bones for medicine. Over thousands of years, more and more sea cows were killed. In some areas, the animal disappeared altogether.

Even today, sea cows are hunted for food in some countries. Wherever they roam, they are in danger of becoming **extinct**, or dying out. For this reason, they are considered **endangered species**.

It is not hunting that endangers the West Indian manatee in the United States. Modern humans have other ways of making life unsafe for the gentle aquatic mammals.

A diver swims alongside a manatee.

The Threats

Like aliens from another planet, people have invaded the manatees' world. We have taken their travel routes as sea lanes for our boats. We have blocked their waterways with flood gates and canal locks that can crush and kill. We have littered their playgrounds with thrown-away fishing lines, hooks, and trash that can snag and choke them.

Our powerful machines have dug canals into their sea grass pastures, and filled in wetlands to make room for buildings. Our chemicals and sewage have **polluted** their world. Even our friendliness has become a threat. Swimmers and divers try to touch the gentle creatures, often driving them from the warmth and safety of winter gathering places.

Most of the manatees in Florida's waters bear propeller scars. But the force of a boat hitting one of them is even more dangerous. A manatee being hit by a large boat is like a person being hit by a truck. In recent years, boats and barges have caused

Swimmers and divers who touch manatees sometimes drive them away from winter gathering places.

at least one-third of the deaths of manatees in Florida. The number has risen as the number of boats has risen. Calves, in particular, find it hard to escape such danger.

Only about 1,200 of the creatures now roam the state's waters. Too many are dying each year. The number of calves that are born and survive to

Propeller scars are visible on the back of this manatee.

become full-grown cannot keep up with the losses.

Will the West Indian manatee go the way of Steller's sea cow? In the United States, government, business, and private groups are working together to make the answer "no." Action is centered in Florida, where the manatees gather.

Protecting the Manatee

Brightly colored signs mark protected waterways in some areas where manatees live in winter. There, boat speeds are limited to prevent injuries. Several warm water gathering spots are set aside as **refuges**, where no boats, swimmers, or divers are allowed. Blue Spring, the winter home of Success, is one such refuge. More are needed, as are more protected waterways.

It is against the law to hunt, capture, kill, or even to disturb or annoy any manatee. But the people who enforce the laws cannot be everywhere the manatees are. Laws, then, are only part of the answer. Educating the public about the gentle giant and its needs is important.

Written materials, classroom talks, television announcements, bumper stickers, and signs all help. There is even a manatee adoption program. People do not get one to take home, but they do get information and pictures so they can learn about one special manatee. Adoption fees help pay for many

Florida's Crystal River Information Center helps educate the public about the needs of the manatee and how it can be protected.

protection efforts led by the Save the Manatee Club.

Research provides information about the manatee's habits and how best to protect it. Florida's Department of Natural Resources (DNR) and the U.S. Fish and Wildlife Service are active in this effort. Scientists attach a radio transmitter to a belt placed above the manatee's tail. In this way they

can track its movements without harm to the animal. They also study the behavior of captive manatees and those in wintering areas. Dead ones are examined to find the cause of death.

Government groups help local planners find ways to meet the needs of growing numbers of

A radio transmitter has been attached to the tail of this manatee.

people without destroying the manatees' homes. Protecting the creatures' habitat is everyone's concern, because the shallow waters are also recreation areas for people. The estuaries and water grass beds are nurseries and homes for much of our seafood. What is good for the manatee, then, is also good for people.

Rescue and Treatment

An injured or sick manatee gets special care. Although the huge, frightened creature often thrashes about wildly, willing hands help lift it onto a type of stretcher. It is transported by truck to the Miami Seaquarium or to Sea World in Orlando. Both are licensed as hospitals for manatees and provide whatever care and treatment are needed.

It is a happy day when a recovered manatee can be returned to the wild. Some can be released in the place they were rescued. For others, DNR's Homosassa Springs State Wildlife Park offers a safe place to adapt to a life of freedom.

Manatees gather around a worker at Homosassa Springs State Wildlife Park.

A program to breed captive manatees for release to the wild is being tried. But it takes a long time for a calf to be born and raised. A Seaquarium manatee named Juliet set a record for captive births when her sixth calf was born. The mother was between 42 and 47 years old and had been captive for

32 years. No one is sure how long a manatee can live or continue to bear young.

Manatees and People

Saving the manatees will not be easy, for it means we humans will have to change some of our ways. Manatees have simple needs, though. If they have plants for food, and are not disturbed, they can live happily in areas close to humans. They are friendly creatures, fascinating to watch. They are just as curious about the strange, two-legged land creatures that invade their world as we are about them.

Everyone who visits areas where manatees live can help in the effort to protect them. We can pick up litter and keep all trash from waters and shores. In particular, we can use care in boats, moving slowly where manatees are known to roam. We can report sightings of manatees with transmitters and of injured or dead manatees. And we can tell others about the remarkable animal that wanders our southern waters.

42

People and manatees can share the warm, shallow water world. We can, and in some areas already do, enjoy each other's presence. Wherever that happens, the world is a better place for both.

Chapter 4

The Story of Success

Hanging motionless near the surface of the water, Success dozes peacefully, her short, broad flippers dangling beneath her. She pays no heed to the sounds around her. The screeches and calls of the seagulls above are familiar. So is the swishing and splashing of the waves. Even the distant hum of motorboats is a sound familiar to her ears.

Suddenly, though, something deep within Success signals an alarm. A rapidly approaching roar triggers frightful memories. Instantly alert, she dives rapidly, just as the hull of a powerful boat passes over her. The knife-sharp blades of the propeller churn the water only inches above her back.

Success has barely escaped the greatest threat to her life and safety. Twice in the past, she had not

In Florida waters, two manatees swim beneath the surface in front of a motorboat.

been so lucky. Then the propeller blades had left deep scars that would be with her always.

She was only a year old the first time. Afterward, her mother's broad flippers and warm milk comforted her as she healed. A year later, though, she had been alone, recently **weaned** from her mother's care. The boat came suddenly then, too. In water too shallow for escape, its hull had crushed her against the bottom. The propeller cut deeply, breaking two of her ribs.

Few manatees survive such severe wounds. But Success was strong and tough. Though stunned and frightened, she forced herself upward for air. Then, pulling along the bottom with her flippers, she found a sheltered, grassy cove. For days she rested there, too weak to eat. Gradually, as the wounds began to heal, she nibbled at the nearby water plants. Slowly, her strength returned.

Now those frightful days are far behind her. She has grown into a large, healthy adult. And she has managed to escape further injury.

A pair of large, full-grown manatees swims side by side.

Blue Spring—A Gathering Place

Pumping her powerful tail, Success quickens her journey toward Blue Spring. Alligators sunning on the water's edge ignore the giant creature as she passes. Schools of silvery fish part as she glides through their midst.

Another manatee approaches. The two nudge

each other, reaching out with their flippers. Success feels the stiff, bristly whiskers of the other as it gently touches her side and back. Rising to the surface, the two touch **muzzles** together. Humans call it a kiss. For the manatees, it is a way of communicating.

Success and the newcomer have met before. Both spend much of the winter at Blue Spring. They travel together along the familiar route, finally passing under the large pipe and bright sign that mark the entrance to Blue Spring Run. No motorboats are allowed in this place of safety and warmth.

A park ranger records their arrival on his note pad. He recognizes most of the more than 50 manatees that visit the spring. Scars, cuts, and other wounds identify each one. Many return yearly, and have been given names.

Sweetgums, Success's mother, has already arrived with a new, healthy calf. Success was the first of her babies to survive, and that was the reason

This sign marks the entrance to the Blue Spring Run manatee preserve along Florida's Saint John's River.

for her name. Her success in surviving the boat attacks makes the name even more fitting.

A Peaceful Life

The first freeze of December brings more of the roly-poly animals to Blue Spring Run. High-pitched squeaks and chirps are exchanged. There is much nudging and nuzzling as they greet each other.

A scientist paddles his canoe overhead, trying to learn more about the manatees' behavior. Success rises to follow the canoe. She rubs against its side, and plays with the paddle. She does not fear this small boat or the person inside it.

Soon, she is ready for her favorite activity—resting. For hours at a time, Success lies on the bottom, dozing. Every few minutes she drifts slowly upward to breathe, then settles back into the same spot. Other manatees, too, are resting, some upside down or on their sides. A few nap at the surface. Life is peaceful, at least for the moment.

Then a young manatee decides to play. He nudges Success, bumping and prodding her until she can ignore him no longer. Soon the two are rolling together in a playful water ballet. Others join in—chasing, rolling, nibbling. They squeal and squeak in the joy of their play.

Thus, the winter passes. Resting, playing, and trips into the nearby river for feeding and exploring

fill the time. When March arrives with its warming winds, journeys away from the spring lengthen. One day, Success and two others leave together. Faraway places beckon. Soon all the manatees will be gone, and only a few will return for summer visits. Many will stay in the river, cruising through

A manatee rests on its side on the bottom.

its many creeks and lakes, stopping to feed wherever water plants abound.

Success and her companions, though, follow the river to the sea, 150 miles (241 kilometers) away. At times, they join one or two others for a few days. Then Success wanders off alone. Her body has grown heavier than usual. She finds a sheltered inlet and waits patiently.

Strange movements flutter within her. Suddenly, she bends her body. Muscles push and pull in her great belly. Then, in the pink dawn of a summer sunrise, a calf is born.

Mother and Calf

Squealing constantly, the newborn rises for air. Success is close beside, and she gives comforting squeals in return. She nuzzles her pudgy, wrinkled calf, then guides it to the underside of her flipper. There her nipple awaits. Warm milk, richer than that of any cow, fills the calf's mouth. Soon the baby tires. Resting on its mother's back, it dozes.

A newborn calf and its mother stay close together, touching almost constantly.

In a few days, Success and her baby swim away, the two touching almost constantly. Success listens to her calf's squeaks as it nudges her broad body.

After several weeks, the calf begins to nibble on sea grasses. But the mother's milk will nourish her for months to come. The young manatee grows rapidly in size and strength. She grows bolder, too.

A calf swims beneath the protective flippers of its mother.

With childlike curiosity, she begins to stray from her mother's side to explore the watery world. A buried log draws her interest. She rubs against it with her belly, back, and tail, scratching herself as she has seen her mother do. Then she finds a large seashell. Rolling it around with her flippers, she lifts it to her mouth. Her lips and tongue examine every inch of the strange object.

But, wait a minute! Where is her mother? The dark water hides her. Frightened screams bring an answering scream as Success rushes to the calf's side. The infant forgets the log and shell as she huddles beneath her mother's flipper.

The months pass quickly as Success teaches her calf the ways of a manatee's life. For almost two years, they will never be far apart. Often they join others, some also with calves. The young manatees play together as their mothers feed or rest.

An early chill reminds Success of Blue Spring. The time has come to lead her calf there. The journey is a slow one, interrupted by lively play between mother and calf.

A pleased ranger records the arrival of the two at Blue Spring Run. He names the new calf Successful. This ends a successful year in the life of a manatee named Success.

Sources of Information
about Manatees

Each manatee, like each person, has its own special habits and ways of behaving. Some are shy, some are bold. One even likes to overturn a scientist's canoe! The Save the Manatee Club has more information about these remarkable creatures, and where they can be seen. It also has lists of reading materials and of the organizations that work to protect the manatee. Most interesting of all is its Adopt-a-Manatee program. Members select one special manatee from Blue Spring or Homosassa Springs and learn more about its life and habits. For information, write to the club at the address listed below.

Save the Manatee Club
500 N. Maitland Avenue
Maitland, Florida 32751

Glossary

adapted—the ability of animals and plants to change in form and habits to become suited to their environment

algae (AL-jee)—a group of plants, such as seaweed and pond scum, found in water and damp places

aquatic (uh-KWAT-ik)—growing or living in water

barnacles—small, hard-shelled sea creatures that attach to various objects, including ship bottoms, rocks, and the skin of manatees and whales

endangered species—kinds of animals and plants that are in danger of becoming extinct

estuaries (ES-chuh-wair-eez)—partly enclosed bodies of water where fresh water from rivers and streams and salt water from the sea meet and mix

extinct—no longer in existence

habitat—the area where a plant or animal naturally lives

herbivorous (huhr-BIH-vohr-us)—feeding mainly on plants

migration—the seasonal movement of animals from one area or climate to another

muzzle—the front part of an animal's head, including its mouth, nose, and jaws

polluted—made unclean or impure

refuge—a place of safety; refuges set aside for manatees and other animals are protected by law

research—careful investigation and study to discover facts about an animal

sirens—in ancient Greek and Roman myths, these were sea maidens who called to sailors with sweet songs

species (SPEE-sheez)—distinct kinds of individual plants or animals that have common characteristics and are classified by scientists as species

weaned—no longer feeding on mother's milk

Index

About the Author

Jean Sibbald's interest in sea life started in childhood when, as the daughter of a marine biologist, she grew up on a marine biological station. Although her career has taken other directions since then, she was and is an avid amateur conchologist. Sibbald is the author of a number of books for young readers, including five in the Ocean World Library.

The author's educational background includes an undergraduate major in biology and a bachelor's and master's degree in speech communication. The mother of two children, she lives in Tampa, Florida.